D1025162

Michael Spötter

A feast in good company

Fondues

Cookery Editor Sonia Allison

Series Editor Wendy Hobson

foulsham

Fondues for all

There is a great deal more to fondue cookery than many people think, and in this appetising and innovative little book, you will find an extravaganza of ideas and recipes for chic and sophisticated fondues made with meat, poultry, offal, game and fish. Most come with their own matching sauces and edible accessories, many have an international flavour and all are designed to see you through warm summer evenings on the patio or lawn to the chill of winter when the best place to be with family and friends is round the intimate warmth of a fondue pot.

Fondues are convivial happenings in gourmet style, an easy way to relax and much less daunting for the cook than a formal meal. Indeed, there is no better way of enjoying a party and no happier way of sharing food and entertainment at the same time. Take it from me and *bon appetit!*

Contents

A Feast from a Single Pot

A fondue is the cosiest way to eat. With everything sizzling on the table, everyone can select a titbit and combine the various pieces to suit individual taste. Then, between each mouthful, there is also plenty of time to enjoy the company of guests and a drink to help the food go down.

Variations on a Theme

Although the non-cheese fondue carries with it a wealth of variations from the point of view of ingredients and accompaniments, the basic techniques of cooking remain the same; either the meat or main ingredient, already cut into bite-sized pieces, is speared on to long fondue forks and sizzled piece by piece in hot oil in the fondue pot until crisp; or it is plunged gently into a pot of simmering, full-flavoured and preferably home-made stock, and cooked to the diner's taste.

Equipment

Fondue sets are readily available from kitchen shops or department stores and each comprises a deep, chimney-shaped pot with stubby handle, a spirit stove over which to place the pot of oil or stock to keep it hot, and a set of long fondue forks. Optional extras include frying baskets, little bowls for the different side dishes and even special plates with divisions from which to eat the meat and accompaniments. While the deep fondue pot, spirit stove and long forks are necessary for success and safety, you can use any dishes and plates to hand for serving. There is no need to spend money on a designer collection.

Tips for Cooking at the Table

* Because of the possibility of drips and spluttering, cover the table first with thick paper then with an easy-to-clean cloth.
* Make sure the fondue pot is within easy reach of the diners. If there are more than six people, you will need two fondue pots; one at each end of the table.
* Use good-quality, neutral-tasting oil, such as corn or sunflower oil, which can reach the high temperature needed for frying. Olive oil is unsuitable.
* To test if the oil is hot enough (around 180°C/350°F) dip in a wooden spoon. If little bubbles form, you can start the fondue.
* Only half fill the pot with oil or stock to prevent overspill and heat conventionally on the hob to bring it up to temperature required (the stock should bubble). Then transfer it to the spirit stove.
* Should the flames go out, *never* try to refill the stove while hot as the spirit itself could catch fire.
* Do not allow too many forks to be submerged into the pot at any one time as the temperature of the oil or stock will fall and the food will only half-cook and might even taste greasy. Likewise, ensure the oil does not begin to overheat and smoke or the stock boil rapidly.
* To make a fondue a satisfying meal, allow 225 g/8 oz to 250 g/9 oz raw ingredients per person.
* Table etiquette demands that each diner puts only one portion of food on to the fork and then into the pot. While that is being eaten (after being transferred to the plate) another piece can be cooking.
* It is usual to season food after cooking as tastes differ. Therefore have pepper and salt available on the table.
* Never eat directly from the fondue forks. Apart from being unhygienic, they become very hot and can burn.
* There is a plentiful selection of recipes for dips and sauces in the book but you can add other items of your choice such as bread, gherkins, silverskin onions, pickled walnuts, pickles, chutney, nuts and yes, even chips.
* If there is any stock left — and it will be quite concentrated by the end of the meal — ladle into little bowls or cups and drink it at the end. If it is too strong, dilute with a little boiling water.

Notes on the Recipes

1 Follow one set of measurements only, do not mix metric and Imperial.
2 Eggs are size 2.
3 Wash fresh produce before preparation.
4 Spoon measurements are level.
5 Adjust seasoning and strongly-flavoured ingredients, such as onions and garlic, to suit your own taste.

6 If you substitute dried for fresh herbs, use only half the amount specified.
7 Preparation times refer to preparation and cooking and are approximate.
8 Kcal and kJs refer to the complete recipe and are approximate.

Cooking Ingredients

In a fondue, the ingredients must cook very quickly so you should buy only the very best quality. The meat should have been properly hung and the vegetables should be young and crisp.

In order to make sure that the meat is really tender, it can be marinated in oil for a few days beforehand and then left to tenderise in the refrigerator. The preparation times given in the recipes do not include this marinating time or maturing time. The calories shown refer to the complete fondue, but do not include sauces or fat.

Pork

The best pork to use for a fondue is fillet, also known as loin. Certain cuts from the leg, the back and the neck can also be used. If desired, tender pieces of meat can be alternated with rashers of streaky bacon, smoked or fresh, to increase flavour and also add contrast.

Veal

Veal is particularly tender and lean. For cooking both in oil and stock, fillet is best but back and leg are also satisfactory. Veal is not always obtainable everywhere and you may have to order it in advance.

Beef

For a fondue, only prime cuts, such as fillet, are recommended. Always marinate your pieces of meat in oil for about eight days, keeping it in the refrigerator. When buying beef, pay particular attention to the quality; let your butcher advise you on what is the best buy.

Lamb

Lamb is a particularly good meat for fondue because it needs a high cooking temperature and gourmets are enthusiastic over its own special taste. Fillet and lamb chops are the best. Cubes can, however, also be cut from leg and shoulder. Look for the pink colour in the flesh of young animals.

Game
A real treat for connoisseurs is boned back of roe-deer, the best cuts from fallow-deer, wild boar or hare fillet. Choose one or more from the selection recommended.

Game poultry
Try this in the autumn during the hunting season, choosing meat from pheasant, wild duck, wild goose and partridge. Game poultry can be found ready to cook in some butchers and meat counters of supermarkets and also in freezer shops.

Poultry
Choose boned leg and breast meat of chicken, duck, turkey and even goose. All are excellent.

Offal
Some offal tastes good cooked in a fondue and you can include liver, kidneys, brains and sweetbreads.

Fish
A meat fondue combined with fish is something special: eel, salmon, sole, turbot, rock salmon, cod, halibut, mussels, prawns – the list of seafood that can be used for fondue is a long one. Have the fish professionally skinned, boned and cut into cubes or strips.

Vegetables
When cooking vegetable fondues, allow about 350 g/12 oz per person. The vegetables should be cubed and blanched beforehand so that the frying or simmering time at the table is short and the vegetables remain crisp. When cooking in oil, the vegetables should be well-drained before cooking, otherwise the fat will spit and splutter too much.

Mushrooms
Cultivated and wild mushrooms take on quite a different taste in the fondue pot; somehow the aroma is much more distinctive and subtle.

Herbs
Use freshly chopped herbs in fondue cookery.

Sauces and Dips

These are classic accompaniments used by diners to add piquancy to the fried or simmered fondue foods. Some can be sprinkled over the cooked food, rather than used as a dip.

Pineapple Foam

Serves 4
Preparation time: 8 mins
570 kcal/2395 kJ

150 ml/¹/₄ pt/²/₃ cup crème fraîche

2 slices pineapple, puréed

a few drops of lemon juice

a few drops of fruit vinegar

a few drops of rum

salt and freshly ground black pepper

a pinch of cayenne pepper

a pinch of sugar

1 Mix the crème fraîche with the pineapple and remaining ingredients in a bowl and whisk until foamy.
2 Season and set aside ready to serve.

Cocktail Sauce

Serves 4
Preparation time: 5 mins
940 kcal/3950 kJ

250 ml/8 fl oz/1 cup mayonnaise

150 ml/¹/₄ pt/²/₃ cup natural yoghurt

20 ml/4 tsp redcurrant jelly, melted

20 ml/4 tsp tomato ketchup

5 ml/1 tsp curry powder

salt and freshly ground black pepper

a pinch of cayenne pepper

a few drops of lemon juice

a few drops of brandy

1 Beat the mayonnaise with the yoghurt, redcurrant jelly and tomato ketchup until smooth.
2 Gently whisk in the remaining ingredients.

Curry Sauce

Serves 4
Preparation time: 5 mins
900 kcal/3780 kJ

150 ml/¹/₄ pt/²/₃ cup crème fraîche

120 ml/4 fl oz/¹/₂ cup mayonnaise

120 ml/4 fl oz/¹/₂ cup dry white wine

a few drops of lemon juice

20 ml/4 tsp soy sauce

10 ml/2 tsp honey

a few drops of Worcestershire sauce

5 ml/1 tsp curry powder

salt and freshly ground black pepper

a pinch of sugar

1 Put the crème fraîche into a bowl with the mayonnaise, wine, lemon juice, soy sauce, honey and Worcestershire sauce. Whisk until foamy.
2 Season well with curry powder, salt, pepper and sugar. Set aside ready to serve.

Dill Cream

Serves 4
Preparation time: 5 mins
450 kcal/1890 kJ

150 ml/¹/₄ pt/²/₃ cup crème fraîche
juice of 1 lemon
a few drops of Worcestershire sauce
a few drops of fruit vinegar
salt and freshly ground black pepper
a pinch of sugar
1 bunch of dill, chopped
a few drops of brandy

1 Whisk the crème fraîche, lemon juice, Worcestershire sauce and fruit vinegar in a bowl until creamy.
2 Season with salt, pepper and sugar and stir in the dill. Add a touch of piquancy with the brandy before serving.

Advocaat Sauce

Serves 4
Preparation time: 5 mins
1390 kcal/5840 kJ

250 ml/8 fl oz/1 cup mayonnaise
250 ml/8 fl oz/1 cup double cream, whipped
145 ml/3 tbsp advocaat
a few drops of Worcestershire sauce
a few drops of fruit vinegar
20 ml/4 tsp chopped cress
salt and freshly ground black pepper
a pinch of sugar

1 Beat the mayonnaise with the cream, advocaat, Worcestershire sauce and fruit vinegar until smooth.
2 Stir in the cress, season and serve as required.

Egg Sauce

Serves 4
Preparation time: 8 mins
1260 kcal/5270 kJ

250 ml/8 fl oz/1 cup mayonnaise
30 ml/2 tbsp double cream
10 ml/2 tsp made mustard
10 ml/2 tsp honey
a few drops of lemon juice
a few drops of fruit vinegar
a few drops of Worcestershire sauce
4 hard-boiled eggs, finely chopped
salt and freshly ground black pepper
5 ml/1 tsp curry powder
a pinch of cayenne pepper

1 Mix the mayonnaise with the cream, mustard, honey, lemon juice, fruit vinegar and Worcester sauce until smooth.
2 Fold in the finely chopped egg then season to taste with salt and pepper. Finally mix in the curry powder and cayenne pepper.

Tangy Honey and Tomato Sauce

Serves 4
Preparation time: 5 mins
340 kcal/1430 kJ

30 ml/**2 tbsp** honey

250 ml/**8 fl oz**/1 cup tomato ketchup

30 ml/**2 tbsp** fruit vinegar

10 ml/**2 tsp** chopped chives

10 ml/**2 tsp** chopped lemon balm

10 ml/**2 tsp** chopped parsley

2 cloves garlic, chopped

2.5 ml/**¹/₂ tsp** cayenne pepper or tabasco sauce

salt and freshly ground black pepper

25 ml/**¹/₂ tsp** curry powder

1 Mix the honey with the ketchup, fruit vinegar, herbs, garlic and the cayenne pepper or tabasco sauce.
2 Season with salt, pepper and curry powder to taste and set aside until ready to serve.

Caviar Sauce

Serves 4
Preparation time: 5 mins
680 kcal/2855 kJ

150 ml/**¹/₄ pt**/²/₃ cup crème fraîche

juice of 1 lemon

a few drops of fruit vinegar

10 ml/**4 tsp** honey

a few drops of sherry

salt and freshly ground black pepper

a pinch of cayenne pepper

45 ml/**3 tbsp** mock caviar

1 Whisk the crème fraîche in a bowl with the lemon juice, fruit vinegar and honey until foamy.
2 Flavour with sherry then season well with salt, pepper and cayenne pepper.
3 Stir the caviar into the sauce before serving.

Garlic Cream

Serves 4
Preparation time: 5 mins
510 kcal/2140 kJ

150 ml/**¹/₄ pt**/²/₃ cup crème fraîche

juice of **¹/₂** lemon

20 ml/**4 tsp** fruit vinegar

5 ml/**1 tsp** salt

4 cloves garlic, finely chopped

freshly ground black pepper

a few drops of Worcestershire sauce

45 ml/**3 tbsp** chopped chives

1 Put the crème fraîche into a bowl with the lemon juice, fruit vinegar, salt and garlic. Whisk until foamy.
2 Season with pepper and Worcestershire sauce, and fold in the chives before serving.

Chinese Garlic Sauce

Serves 4
Preparation time: 8 mins
860 kcal/3610 kJ

---

4 cloves garlic

5 ml/*1 tsp* salt

1 bunch of parsley, chopped

1 bunch of chives, chopped

20 ml/*4 tsp* honey

juice of 1 lemon

250 ml/*8 fl oz*/1 cup rice wine or dry sherry

20 ml/*4 tsp* soy sauce

20 ml/*4 tsp* sesame oil

2 hard-boiled eggs, chopped

salt and freshly ground black pepper

---

1 Crush the garlic cloves with the salt. Put them into a bowl and beat in the herbs, honey, lemon juice, rice wine and the soy sauce.
2 Beat in the sesame oil a drop at a time. Fold in the eggs, season with salt and pepper and serve.

Crab Cream

Serves 4
Preparation time: 8 mins
1290 kcal/5420 kJ

---

250 ml/*8 fl oz*/1 cup mayonnaise

250 ml/*8 fl oz*/1 cup crème fraîche

75 g/*3 oz* crab meat, puréed

a few drops of lemon juice

a few drops of fruit vinegar

a few drops of Worcestershire sauce

salt and freshly ground black pepper

a pinch of sugar

a pinch of cayenne pepper

---

1 Whisk the mayonnaise with the crème fraîche until foamy.
2 Fold in the crab meat. Flavour with lemon juice, fruit vinegar and Worcestershire sauce, then season to taste with salt, pepper, sugar and cayenne pepper.

Herb Cream

Serves 4
Preparation time: 5 mins
1190 kcal/4995 kJ

---

250 ml/*8 fl oz*/1 cup mayonnaise

250 ml/*8 fl oz*/1 cup crème fraîche

juice of 1 lemon

10 ml/*4 tsp* chopped parsley

10 ml/*4 tsp* chopped chives

10 ml/*4 tsp* chopped lemon balm

a few drops of Worcestershire sauce

a pinch of sugar

salt and freshly ground black pepper

---

1 Whisk the mayonnaise, crème fraîche and lemon juice in a bowl until foamy.
2 Fold in the chopped herbs and season to taste with Worcestershire sauce, sugar, salt and pepper.

Fine Herb Sauce

Serves 4
Preparation time: 5 mins
390 kcal/1640 kJ

250 ml/8 fl oz/1 cup white wine

20 ml/4 tsp olive oil

20 ml/4 tsp chopped parsley

20 ml/4 tsp chopped chives

20 ml/4 tsp chopped lemon balm

2 cloves garlic finely chopped

20 ml/4 tsp wine vinegar

10 ml/2 tsp medium-sharp made mustard

1 hard-boiled egg, chopped

salt and freshly ground black pepper

a pinch of sugar

1 Mix the wine with the olive oil, herbs, garlic, wine vinegar, mustard and egg.
2 Season to taste with salt, pepper and sugar.

Horseradish Sauce

Serves 4
Preparation time: 5 mins
1120 kcal/4705 kJ

150 ml/¹/₄ pt/²/₃ cup double cream

120 ml/4 fl oz/¹/₂ cup mayonnaise

20 ml/4 tsp finely grated horseradish or horseradish sauce

juice of ¹/₂ lemon

a few drops of Worcestershire sauce

salt and freshly ground black pepper

a pinch of sugar

1 Whisk the cream until stiff then mix in the mayonnaise, horseradish and lemon juice.
2 Add the Worcestershire sauce and season to taste with salt, pepper and sugar.

Pepper Sauce

Serves 4
Preparation time: 5 mins
910 kcal/3820 kJ

250 ml/8 fl oz/1 cup mayonnaise

150 ml/¹/₄ pt/²/₃ cup natural yoghurt

juice of ¹/₂ lemon

30 ml/2 tbsp redcurrant jelly, melted

20 ml/4 tbsp green peppercorns

a few drops of brandy

15 ml/1 tbsp chopped parsley

15 ml/1 tbsp chopped chives

1 Blend the mayonnaise with yoghurt, lemon juice and redcurrant jelly until smooth.
2 Stir in the peppercorns and flavour with brandy. Fold in the herbs.

Cranberry Cream

Serves 4
Preparation time: 5 mins
900 kcal/3780 kJ

---

150 ml/¹/₄ pt/²/₃ cup double cream

45 ml/3 tbsp cranberry jelly or sauce

a few drops of lemon juice

a few drops of brandy

salt and freshly ground black pepper

1 Whip the cream until stiff then fold in the cranberry jelly or sauce.
2 Season with lemon juice, brandy, salt and pepper.

Remoulade Sauce

Serves 4
Preparation time: 5 mins
1390 kcal/5840 kJ

---

375 ml/13 fl oz/1¹/₂ cups mayonnaise

120 ml/4 fl oz/¹/₂ cup crème fraîche

1 onion, finely chopped

1 pickled gherkin, finely chopped

1 caper, finely chopped

4-5 anchovy fillets, finely chopped

20 ml/4 tsp chopped chives

20 ml/4 tsp chopped parsley

20 ml/4 tsp chopped chervil

20 ml/4 tsp chopped tarragon

10 ml/2 tsp made mustard

juice of ¹/₂ lemon

a pinch of sugar

salt and freshly ground black pepper

1 Mix the mayonnaise with the crème fraîche. Stir in the onion, gherkin, caper and anchovy fillets.
2 Fold in the herbs, mustard and lemon juice. Season to taste with the remaining ingredients.

Roquefort Sauce

Serves 4
Preparation time: 5 mins
870 kcal/3655 kJ

---

100 g/4 oz full-fat soft cream cheese

60 ml/4 tbsp crème fraîche

15 ml/1 tbsp double cream

50 g/2 oz Roquefort or blue veined cheese, crumbled

a few drops of lemon juice

a few drops of Worcestershire sauce

a pinch of sugar

salt and freshly ground black pepper

a few drops of Kirsch

20 ml/4 tsp chopped parsley

1 Beat the cream cheese, crème fraîche, cream and blue cheese in a bowl and beat until foamy and evenly blended.
2 Season well with lemon juice, Worcestershire sauce, sugar, salt and pepper.
3 Flavour with Kirsch then fold in the parsley.

Chive Sauce

Serves 4
Preparation time: 5 mins
1190 kcal/5000 kJ

---

250 ml/8 fl oz/1 cup mayonnaise

250 ml/8 fl oz/1 cup double cream, whipped

1 bunch of chives, chopped

a few drops of lemon juice

a few drops of Worcestershire sauce

a few drops of brandy

salt and freshly ground black pepper

a pinch of sugar

a pinch of nutmeg

1 Mix the mayonnaise with the cream then fold in the chives.
2 Flavour with lemon juice and Worcestershire sauce then add the remaining ingredients.

Mustard Sauce

Serves 4
Preparation time: 5 mins
1200 kcal/5040 kJ

---

250 ml/8 fl oz/1 cup crème fraîche

250 ml/8 fl oz/1 cup mayonnaise

15 ml/1 tbsp made mustard

juice of ¹/₂ lemon

a few drops of Worcestershire sauce

a pinch of sugar

salt and freshly ground black pepper

30 ml/2 tbsp chopped chives

1 Whisk the crème fraîche smoothly with the mayonnaise, mustard and lemon juice.
2 Season well then fold in the chives.

Bacon Sauce

Serves 4
Preparation time: 8 mins
680 kcal/2855 kJ

---

2 thick rashers streaky bacon, finely chopped

20 ml/4 tsp corn oil

1 onion, chopped

1 leek, cut into strips

1 clove garlic, chopped

250 ml/8 fl oz/1 cup dry white wine

30 ml/2 tbsp tarragon vinegar

250 ml/8 fl oz/1 cup chopped mixed herbs

salt and freshly ground black pepper

a pinch of sugar

1 Fry the bacon in the oil until soft.
2 Add the onion, leek and garlic and fry gently for a few minutes.
3 Pour on the white wine, add the tarragon vinegar and simmer over a moderate heat for 5-6 minutes.
4 Remove the pan from the heat and stir in the herbs. Season with the remaining ingredients. Serve hot or warm.

Tzatziki

Serves 4
Preparation time: 5 mins
540 kcal/2270 kJ

100 g/4 oz low fat quark
150 ml/¼ pt/⅔ cup soured cream
5 ml/1 tsp salt
2 garlic cloves, crushed
100 g/4 oz cucumber, finely diced
juice of ½ lemon
5 ml/1 tsp sugar
salt and freshly ground black pepper
30 ml/2 tbsp chopped chives

1 Mix the quark with the soured cream, salt and garlic.
2 Fold in the cucumber and stir in remaining ingredients.

Brandied Cranberries

Serves 4
Preparation time: 5 mins
480 kcal/2015 kJ

225 g/8 oz cranberry sauce
30 ml/2 tbsp brandy
a few drops of lemon juice
salt
a pinch of cayenne pepper

1 Mix the cranberry sauce with the brandy and lemon juice. Season well to taste and stir until the ingredients are smoothly blended.

Lemon Sauce

Serves 4
Preparation time: 5 mins
840 kcal/3530 kJ

150 ml/¼ pt/⅔ cup crème fraîche
120 ml/4 fl oz/½ cup mayonnaise
1 small onion, finely grated
15 ml/1 tsp lemon juice
8 leaves of lemon balm, finely chopped
a pinch of sugar
salt and freshly ground black pepper

1 Mix the crème fraîche with the mayonnaise, onion and lemon juice until smooth.
2 Stir in the lemon balm. Season to taste with the remaining ingredients.

Bubbling and Sizzling

This section deals with fondues in which the food – meat, poultry and vegetables – is fried in oil in a pot over a spirit stove to give a tender mouthful with a crispy outside. See page 6 on cooking tips.

Farmer's Fondue, page 20

Farmer's Fondue

Serves 4
Preparation time: 35 mins
plus marinating
2050 kcal/8610 kJ

1 kg/2¼ lb pork spare ribs

120 ml/4 fl oz/½ cup corn oil

120 ml/4 fl oz/½ cup beer

150 ml/¼ pt/⅔ cup tomato ketchup

15 ml/1 tbsp curry powder

10 ml/2 tsp green peppercorns

1 chilli pepper, seeds removed and chopped

2 cloves garlic, chopped

20 ml/4 tsp black treacle

20 ml/4 tsp red wine vinegar

5 ml/1 tsp paprika

10 ml/2 tsp chopped marjoram

5 ml/1 tsp chopped thyme

1 dish Egg Sauce (p11)

1 dish Fine Herb Sauce (p14)

1 dish Pepper Sauce (p14)

1 dish mixed pickles

1 dish chopped herbs

oil or vegetable fat for frying

1 Chop the spare ribs into pieces.
2 Beat the oil, beer, ketchup, curry powder, peppercorns, chilli, garlic, treacle, wine vinegar, spices and herbs.
3 Pour this over the ribs and mix. Cover and refrigerate for 5 hours, turning occasionally. Drain.
4 Arrange the meat and side dishes on plates. Heat the oil, pour it into the fondue pot, and serve.

Photograph page 18

20

Picnic Fondue

Serves 4
Preparation time: 30 mins
plus marinating
3880 kcal/16295 kJ

300 g/1 oz lean pork

300 g/1 oz belly of pork

4 frankfurters

250 ml/8 fl oz/1 cup tomato ketchup

120 ml/4 fl oz/½ cup wine vinegar

30 ml/2 tbsp honey

2 cloves garlic, chopped

5 ml/1 tsp chopped marjoram

5 ml/1 tsp chopped thyme

10 ml/2 tsp grated lemon rind

5 ml/1 tsp paprika

5 ml/1 tsp curry powder

a pinch of cayenne pepper

1 dish Herb Cream (p13)

1 dish Brandied Cranberries (p17)

1 dish Mustard Sauce (p16)

oil or vegetable fat for frying

1 Cut the meat and sausages into bite-sized pieces.
2 Mix together the ketchup, oil, wine vinegar, honey, garlic, herbs, lemon rind and spices.
3 Pour this marinade over the meats and mix. Cover and the refrigerate for 5 hours, turning occasionally. Drain.
4 Arrange the meats and side dishes on plates. Heat the oil, pour it into the fondue pot, and serve.

Photograph opposite (top)

Fiery Lamb Fondue

Serves 4
Preparation time: 40 mins
plus marinating
1420 kcal/5965 kJ

450 g/1 lb lamb fillet

150 ml/¼ pt/⅔ cup olive or corn oil

5 ml/1 tsp salt

2 cloves garlic, chopped

10 ml/2 tsp grated lemon rind

5 ml/1 tsp cayenne pepper

5 ml/1 tsp chopped thyme

5 ml/1 tsp chopped rosemary

60 ml/4 tbsp chopped mint

5 ml/1 tsp freshly ground black pepper

1 dish Garlic Cream (p12)

1 dish Herb Cream (p13)

1 dish Tzatziki (p17)

oil or vegetable fat for frying

1 Cut the meat into cubes and place in a bowl.
2 Beat together the oil, salt, garlic, lemon rind, cayenne pepper, herbs and black pepper to make a marinade.
3 Pour the marinade over the lamb and mix thoroughly. Cover and leave in the refrigerator for 4 hours, turning occasionally. Drain.
4 Arrange the meat and side dishes on serving plates. Heat the oil, pour it into the fondue pot, and serve.

Photograph opposite (bottom)

21

Beef Fondue

Serves 4
Preparation time: 25 mins
plus marinating
1220 kcal/5125 kJ

300 g/*11 oz* beef fillet
300 g/*11 oz* rump steak
250 ml/*8 fl oz*/1 cup olive oil
20 ml/*4 tsp* soy sauce
10 ml/*2 tsp* honey
5 ml/*1 tsp* salt
1 clove garlic, crushed
10 ml/*2 tsp* chopped marjoram
10 ml/*2 tsp* chopped thyme
grated rind of *¹/₂* a lemon
a pinch of cayenne pepper
a few drops of brandy
salt and freshly ground black pepper
1 dish Advocaat Sauce (p11)
1 dish Lemon Sauce (p17)
1 dish Herb Cream (p13)
1 dish chopped nuts
oil or vegetable fat for frying

1 Cut the meat into cubes and place in a bowl.
2 Mix together the oil, soy sauce, honey, salt, garlic, the herbs and lemon rind. Season with cayenne pepper, brandy, salt and pepper.
3 Pour this marinade over the meat and mix. Cover and chill for 5 hours, turning occasionally.
4 Arrange the meat and side dishes on plates. Heat the oil, pour it into the fondue pot and serve.

Photograph (left)

Best Fillet Fondue

Serves 4
Preparation time: 30 mins
plus marinating
1290 kcal/5420 kJ

225 g/**8 oz** beef fillet	
225 g/**8 oz** pork fillet	
225 g/**8 oz** veal fillet	
225 g/**8 oz** lamb fillet	
250 ml/**8 fl oz**/1 cup olive oil	
5 ml/**1 tsp** salt	
2 cloves garlic, chopped	
20 ml/**4 tsp** green peppercorns	
10 ml/**2 tsp** herbs de Provence	
45 ml/**3 tbsp** brandy	
1 dish Cocktail Sauce (p10)	
1 dish Fine Herb Sauce (p14)	
1 dish Garlic Cream (p12)	
1 dish chopped peanuts	
1 dish chopped mixed herbs	
oil or vegetable fat for frying	

1 Cut the meat into cubes and place in a bowl.
2 Mix together the oil, salt, garlic, peppercorns, herbs and brandy to make a marinade.
3 Pour the marinade over the meat and mix thoroughly. Cover and leave in the refrigerator for 5 hours, turning occasionally. Drain.
4 Arrange the meat and side dishes on serving plates. Heat the oil, pour it into the fondue pot and serve.

Photograph (right)

Minced Meat Fondue

Serves 4
Preparation time: 35 mins
1910 kcal/8020 kJ

300 g/11 oz minced beef

300 g/11 oz minced pork

1 onion, finely chopped

120 ml/4 fl oz/¹/₂ cup milk

2 slices white bread, crumbed

2 eggs, beaten

5 ml/1 tsp salt

2 cloves garlic, crushed

20 ml/4 tsp made mustard

a pinch of cayenne pepper

5 ml/1 tsp chopped marjoram

5 ml/1 tsp chopped thyme

¹/₂ bunch of parsley, chopped

1 dish Garlic Cream (p12)

1 dish Egg Sauce (p11)

1 dish mixed pickles

oil or vegetable fat for frying

1 Knead meats smoothly with the onion, milk, breadcrumbs, eggs, salt, garlic, mustard, cayenne pepper, marjoram, thyme and parsley, and shape the mixture into little dumplings.
2 Arrange the dumplings and side dishes on serving plates. Heat the oil, pour it into the fondue pot and serve.

Photograph (left)

Titbit Fondue

Serves 4
Preparation time: 45 mins
1010 kcal/4240 kJ

150 g/5 oz beef fillet

150 g/5 oz calves' heart

150 g/5 oz veal kidney

150 g/5 oz calves' liver

2 carrots, diced

225 g/8 oz cauliflower florets

200 g/7 oz Brussels sprouts

250 ml/8 fl oz/1 cup vegetable stock

1 dish Fine Herb Sauce (p14)

1 dish Brandied Cranberries (p17)

1 dish Pepper Sauce (p14)

1 dish chopped peanuts

oil or vegetable fat for frying

1 Cut the meat into strips or cubes. Skin the kidney and the liver, clean well and cut up in the same way as the meat.
2 Cook the vegetables in the stock until tender, then remove and leave to drain until dry.
3 Arrange the meat, vegetables and side dishes on serving plates. Heat the oil, pour it into the fondue pot, and serve.

Photograph (left)

Rustic Fondue

Serves 4
Preparation time: 40 mins
plus marinating
2450 kcal/10290 kJ

---

8 small lamb chops

150 g/5 oz lamb fillet

2 cloves garlic, chopped

5 ml/1 tsp chopped thyme

5 ml/1 tsp chopped marjoram

5 ml/1 tsp chopped mint

45 ml/3 tbsp olive oil

4 frying sausages, either pork or beef

8-12 cherry tomatoes

1 red pepper, diced

1 green pepper, diced

1 dish Herb Cream (p13)

1 dish Mustard Sauce (p16)

1 dish Horseradish Sauce (p14)

oil or vegetable fat for frying

1 Cut the lamb chops into two and the fillets into cubes, and place in a bowl.
2 Mix together the garlic, thyme, marjoram, mint and oil and rub well into the meat. Cover and leave in the refrigerator for at least 30 minutes.
3 Cut the sausages into little chunks.
4 Arrange the meat, sausages, vegetables and side dishes on serving plates. Heat the oil, pour it into the fondue pot, and serve.

Photograph opposite (top left)

Pork Trotter Fondue

Serves 4
Preparation time: 45 mins
2210 kcal/9280 kJ

---

300 g/11 oz boiled or roasted pig's trotter

300 g/11 oz frying steak

4 chicken drumsticks, boned

salt and freshly ground black pepper

100 g/4 oz/1 cup plain flour

2 eggs, beaten

225 g/8 oz/2 cups toasted breadcrumbs

grated rind of ¹/₂ lemon

4 carrots, sliced

4 onions, sliced

1 dish Remoulade Sauce (p15)

1 dish Chive Sauce (p16)

1 dish Lemon Sauce (p17)

1 dish Tzatziki (p17)

oil or vegetable fat for frying

1 Cut the trotter, steak and chicken into cubes and season with salt and pepper.
2 Coat the pieces in the flour then the beaten eggs. Mix the breadcrumbs with lemon peel, then toss the meat in the crumbs.
3 Arrange the meat, chicken, vegetables and side dishes on serving plates. Heat the oil, pour it into the fondue pot and serve.

Photograph opposite (top right)

Hunter's Fondue

Serves 4
Preparation time: 40 mins
1360 kcal/5710 kJ

---

2 back fillets of hare

2 pheasant breasts

300 g/11 oz venison fillet

a few drops of brandy

10 ml/2 tsp finely ground peppercorns

5 ml/1 tsp finely ground juniper berries

225 g/8 oz oyster mushrooms

225 g/8 oz mixed woodland mushrooms (chantrelle, chestnut) or button mushrooms

juice of 1 lemon

30 ml/2 tbsp cornflour

1 dish Pepper Sauce (p14)

1 dish Cranberry Cream (p15)

1 dish Cocktail Sauce (p10)

1 dish Fine Herb Sauce (p14)

1 dish chopped hazelnuts

oil or vegetable fat for frying

1 Cube the meats.
2 Sprinkle with brandy and rub in the peppercorns and juniper berries.
3 Chop the woodland mushrooms or leave button mushrooms whole. Sprinkle with lemon juice and toss in the cornflour.
4 Arrange the meat, mushrooms and side dishes on serving plates. Heat the oil, pour it into the fondue pot, and serve.

Photograph opposite (bottom)

Beer Batter Fondue

Serves 4
Preparation time: 50 mins
plus marinating
2330 kcal/9785 kJ

150 g/5 oz beef fillet

2 chicken breast fillets

150 g/5 oz pork fillet

45 ml/3 tbsp olive oil

2 cloves garlic, chopped

5 ml/1 tsp salt

5 ml/1 tsp chopped oregano

5 ml/1 tsp chopped basil

a few drops of brandy

150 g/5 oz fish fillet such as
haddock or sole

a few drops of lemon juice

a few drops of
Worcestershire sauce

150 g/5 oz cauliflower florets

150 g/5 oz broccoli florets

Beer batter:

200 g/7 oz flour

a pinch of salt

300 ml/¹/₂ pint/1 ¹/₄ cups
Guinness

10 ml/2 tsp olive oil

2 eggs, separated

1 dish Herb Cream (p13)

1 dish Remoulade Sauce
(p15)

1 dish Horseradish Sauce
(p14)

1 dish Cranberry Cream
(p15)

oil or vegetable fat for frying

1 Cut the beef, chicken and pork into cubes and place in a bowl.
2 Mix together the olive oil, garlic, salt, oregano, basil and brandy to make a marinade.
3 Pour the marinade over the meat, mix thoroughly. Cover and leave in the refrigerator for at least 1 hour. Drain.
4 Wash and dry the fish, then cut into cubes. Sprinkle with lemon juice and Worcestershire sauce, cover and leave in the refrigerator for 10 minutes.
5 Blanch the vegetables in boiling salted water for 3 minutes, remove and allow to drain well.
6 To make the batter, sift the flour and salt into a bowl. Beat in the Guinness, olive oil and egg yolks until smooth.
7 Whisk the egg whites until very stiff and fold into the batter with a metal spoon.
8 Arrange the meat, fish, vegetables and side dishes on serving plates. Place the beer batter in a bowl. Heat the oil, pour it into the fondue pot and serve.
9 To cook, spear the meat on to the fondue fork then dip it into the beer batter. Allow the surplus to drip off and then cook in the hot oil.

Photograph opposite (top)

Poultry Fondue

Serves 4
Preparation time: 50 mins
1720 kcal/7225 kJ

2 chicken breast fillets

2 duck breast fillets

2 pheasant breast fillets

100 g/4 oz broccoli florets

100 g/4 oz carrots, diced

100 g/4 oz celery, diced

100 g/4 oz mushrooms

a few drops of lemon juice

a few drops Worcestershire
sauce

salt and freshly ground
black pepper

30 ml/2 tbsp cornflour

1 dish Herb Cream (p13)

1 dish Egg Sauce (p11)

1 dish Pineapple Foam
(p10)

oil or vegetable fat for frying

1 Cut the poultry into pieces.
2 Blanch the vegetables in boiling salted water until soft, remove and drain thoroughly.
3 Sprinkle the mushrooms with lemon juice and Worcestershire sauce.
4 Season the vegetables with salt and pepper and dust with the cornflour.
5 Arrange the poultry, vegetables and side dishes on serving plates. Heat the oil, pour it into the fondue pot and serve.

Photograph opposite (bottom)

Greek Fondue

Serves 4
Preparation time: 50 mins
1610 kcal/8890 kJ

---

150 g/5 oz lamb fillet

150 g/5 oz chicken breast fillet

300 g/11 oz minced lamb

1 onion, chopped

1 egg, beaten

30 ml/2 tbsp breadcrumbs

1 clove garlic, chopped

5 ml/1 tsp paprika

salt and freshly ground black pepper

5 ml/1 tsp chopped mint

1 red pepper, diced

1 green pepper, diced

1 small aubergine, diced

2 small courgettes, diced

1 dish Tzatziki (p17)

1 dish Herb Cream (p13)

1 dish Fine Herb Sauce (p14)

1 dish chopped nuts

1 dish chopped mixed herbs

oil or vegetable fat for frying

---

1 Cut the meats into cubes. Work the minced lamb to a smooth paste with the onion, egg, breadcrumbs, garlic, salt, pepper and mint. Form the mixture into little balls.
2 Arrange the meat, meatballs, vegetables and side dishes on serving plates. Heat the oil, pour it into the fondue pot, and serve.

Photograph (left)

30

Pork and Vegetable Fondue

Serves 4
Preparation time: 40 mins
1240 kcal/5210 kJ

450 g/1 lb pork fillet
150 g/5 oz tofu
150 g/5 oz cauliflower florets
150 g/5 oz broccoli florets
150 g/5 oz carrots, diced
150 g/5 oz spring onions, cut into 2 cm/1 in pieces
100 g/4 oz mushrooms, thickly sliced
juice of 1 lemon
a few drops of Worcestershire sauce
45 ml/3 tbsp cornflour
salt and freshly ground black pepper
1 dish Herb Cream (p13)
1 dish Mustard Sauce (p16)
1 dish Egg Sauce (p11)
1 dish Tzatziki (p17)
1 dish chopped herbs
oil or vegetable fat for frying

1 Cut the pork and tofu into cubes.
2 Blanch the vegetables in boiling salted water or stock until just soft. Drain.
3 Sprinkle the mushrooms with lemon juice and Worcester sauce.
4 Dust the vegetables with cornflour and season with salt and pepper.
5 Arrange the meat, tofu, vegetables and side dishes on serving plates. Heat the oil, pour into the fondue pot, and serve.

Photograph (right)

Veal Fondue

Serves 4
Preparation time: 45 mins
1890 kcal/7940 kJ

600 g/1¼ lb minced veal
1 small onion, minced
60 ml/4 tbsp milk
2 slices white bread, crumbed
2 eggs, beaten
30 ml/2 tbsp crème fraîche
juice of 1 lemon
a few drops of Worcestershire sauce
salt and freshly ground black pepper
a pinch of cayenne pepper
½ bunch of parsley, chopped
45 ml/3 tbsp breadcrumbs (optional)
1 dish Lemon Sauce (p17)
1 dish Pineapple Foam (p10)
1 dish Mustard Sauce (p16)
1 dish Caviar Sauce (p12)
1 dish chopped peanuts
oil or vegetable fat for frying

1 Mix together the veal, onion, milk, bread, eggs, crème fraîche, lemon juice, Worcestershire sauce, salt, pepper, cayenne and parsley.
2 With damp hands, form the mixture into little balls.
3 Arrange the meatballs and side dishes on serving plates. Heat the oil, pour it into the fondue pot, and serve.

Photograph (top left)

Country Fondue

Serves 4
Preparation time: 30 mins
1230 kcal/5160 kJ

2 chicken breast fillets
2 turkey breast fillets
juice of 2 lemons
a few drops of Worcestershire sauce
salt and freshly ground black pepper
30 ml/2 tbsp cornflour
2 onions, diced
4 carrots, diced
1 dish Dill Cream (p11)
1 dish Lemon Sauce (p17)
1 dish Mustard Sauce (p16)
1 dish chopped mixed herbs
oil or vegetable fat for frying

1 Cut the poultry fillets into cubes and place in a bowl.
2 Sprinkle the fillets with lemon juice and Worcestershire sauce, season with salt and pepper and leave in the refrigerator for 10 minutes.
3 Dust the fillets with cornflour.
4 Arrange the meat cubes, vegetables and side dishes on serving plates. Heat the oil, pour it into the fondue pot, and serve.

Photograph (bottom)

Celebration Fondue

Serves 4
Preparation time: 40 mins
820 kcal/3445 kJ

---

150 g/*5 oz* large shelled prawns

150 g/*5 oz* shelled mussels

150 g/*5 oz* veal fillet, cubed

juice of 2 lemons

Worcestershire sauce

salt and freshly ground black pepper

a few drops of brandy

2 cloves garlic, chopped

60 ml/*4 tbsp* chopped mixed herbs

30 ml/*2 tbsp* cornflour

1 dish Garlic Cream (p12)

1 dish Caviar Sauce (p12)

1 dish Cocktail Sauce (p10)

1 dish Dill Cream (p11)

oil or vegetable fat for frying

---

1 Place the shellfish and veal in a bowl. Sprinkle with lemon juice and Worcestershire sauce and season with salt and pepper. Flavour with brandy then stir in the garlic and herbs. Cover and leave in the refrigerator for 10 minutes.
2 Take out the shellfish and meat, dust with cornflour and arrange on serving plates.
3 Arrange the side dishes on serving plates. Heat the oil, pour it into the fondue pot, and serve.

Photograph opposite (top left)

Gourmet Fondue

Serves 4
Preparation time: 50 mins
1860 kcal/7810 kJ

---

150 g/*5 oz* beef fillet

150 g/*5 oz* lamb fillet

150 g/*5 oz* pork fillet

8 medium-sized lobster tails

100 g/*4 oz* broccoli florets

100 g/*4 oz* carrots, cut into strips

200 g/*7 oz* French or kidney beans

8-12 rashers streaky bacon

1 dish Cocktail Sauce (p10)

1 dish Caviar Sauce (p12)

1 dish Herb Cream (p13)

1 dish Egg Sauce (p11)

1 dish Pepper Sauce (p14)

oil or vegetable fat for frying

---

1 Cut the meat into cubes or strips. Wash the lobster tails in running water and drain well.
2 Blanch the vegetables quickly in boiling salt water, then drain thoroughly.
3 Divide the beans into 8 or 12 bundles and wrap a bacon rasher round each.
4 Arrange the meat, lobster, vegetables and side dishes on serving plates. Heat the oil, pour it into the fondue pot and serve.

Photograph opposite (top right)

Trieste Fondue

Serves 4
Preparation time: 55 mins
plus marinating
1460 kcal/6130 kJ

---

750 g/*1 1/2 lb* pork fillet

2 cloves garlic, crushed

5 ml/*1 tsp* salt

5 ml/*1 tsp* grated lemon rind

5 ml/*1 tsp* chopped thyme

5 ml/*1 tsp* chopped basil

250 ml/*8 fl oz/1 cup* olive oil

a few drops of lemon juice

a few drops of Worcestershire sauce

1 dish Cocktail Sauce (p10)

1 dish Curry Sauce (p10)

1 dish Herb Cream (p13)

1 dish Lemon Sauce (p17)

1 dish toasted chopped almonds

1 dish chopped mixed herbs

oil or vegetable fat for frying

---

1 Cut the pork into slices and place in a bowl.
2 Mix together the garlic, salt, lemon rind, herbs and olive oil to make a marinade.
3 Sprinkle the meat with lemon juice and Worcestershire sauce. Pour the marinade over the meat and mix thoroughly. Cover and refrigerate for at least 1 hour, turning occasionally.
4 Arrange the meat and side dishes on plates. Heat the oil, pour it into the fondue pot, and serve.

Photograph opposite (bottom)

Simmering and Boiling

Fondues cooked in stock are part of everyday life in Asia. The ingredients release a delicious aroma in the gently simmering broth, and the greater the variety with which they are chosen, the better the broth will taste afterwards. If there is a good combination in the fondue stock pot – including meat, fish and vegetables – you will be surprised at how good it tastes.

Sweet and Sour Onion Fondue, page 38

Sweet and Sour Onion Fondue

Serves 4
Preparation time: 40 mins
4080 kcal/17055 kJ

150 g/5 oz pork fillet
150 g/5 oz lamb fillet
225 g/8 oz kabanos
225 g/8 oz pork sausagemeat
1 egg
30 ml/2 tbsp breadcrumbs
20 ml/4 tsp chopped mixed herbs
1 glass dry white wine
750 ml/1 1/4 pts/3 cups meat stock for simmering
a dash of wine vinegar
3 onions, sliced
2 bay leaves
a few cloves
a few mustard seeds
a few peppercorns
15 ml/1 tbsp brown sugar
salt and freshly ground black pepper
1 dish Garlic Cream (p12)
1 dish Mustard Sauce (p16)
1 dish mixed pickles

1 Cut the pork and lamb into thin strips and the kabanos into slices. Combine the sausagemeat with the egg, breadcrumbs and herbs and shape into little balls.
2 Heat the white wine, stock and vinegar and pour it into the fondue pot. Add the onions, bay leaves, cloves, mustard seeds and sugar and simmer for 8 to 10 minutes. Season to taste with salt and pepper.
3 Arrange the meat, sausage, meat balls and side dishes on serving plates and serve with the stock.

Photograph page 36

Gourmet Tip
Other vegetables may be added to the stock while simmering and these include leeks, red and green peppers, fennel and celery.

Fine Ham Fondue

Serves 4
Preparation time: 45 mins
2890 kcal/12140 kJ

150 g/5 oz boiled ham
150 g/5 oz uncooked gammon
150 g/5 oz smoked pork loin
150 g/5 oz veal fillet
4 baby leeks, cut into pieces
225 g/8 oz mushrooms
a few drops of lemon juice
1 glass dry white wine
500 ml/18 fl oz/2 1/4 cups meat stock for simmering
1 onion, studded with cloves
150 ml/1/4 pt/2/3 cup whipping cream
salt and freshly ground black pepper
1 dish of Roquefort Sauce (p15)
1 dish Chive Sauce (p16)
1 dish mixed pickles

1 Cut the ham, gammon, pork and veal into cubes.
2 Sprinkle the leeks and mushrooms with lemon juice.
3 Put the wine, stock, onion and cream in the fondue pot and simmer for about 5 to 8 minutes. Season to taste with salt and pepper.
4 Arrange meat, vegetables and side dishes on serving plates and serve with the stock.

Photograph opposite

Supper Fondue

Serves 4
Preparation time: 45 mins
3830 kcal/16085 kJ

150 g/*5 oz* salami	
4 frankfurters	
4 turkey sausages	
225 g/*8 oz* pork or beef sausagemeat	
1 egg, beaten	
30 ml/*2 tbsp* breadcrumbs	
2 onions, diced	
2 carrots, diced	
1 red pepper, diced	
1 green pepper, diced	
1 glass beer	
750 ml/1 1/4 *pts*/3 cups meat stock for simmering	
a dash of vinegar	
15 ml/*1 tbsp* golden syrup	
10 ml/*2 tsp* chopped marjoram	
salt and freshly ground black pepper	
1 dish Mustard Sauce (p16)	
1 dish Horseradish Sauce (p14)	
1 dish Pepper Sauce (p14)	

1 Slice the sausages.
2 Mix the sausagemeat, egg and breadcrumbs and shape into small balls.
3 Place the beer, stock, vinegar, syrup and marjoram in the fondue pot and simmer for 5 to 8 minutes over a moderate heat. Season to taste.
4 Arrange the vegetables, sausages, meatballs and side dishes on plates and serve with the stock.

Photograph (left)

Meat-Asparagus Fondue

Serves 4
Preparation time: 55 mins
2410 kcal/10120 kJ

150 g/**5 oz** beef fillet	
150 g/**5 oz** veal fillet	
150 g/**5 oz** boiled ham	
150 g/**5 oz** gammon	
400 g/**14 oz** fresh asparagus, blanched	
1 glass dry white wine	
750 ml/1 ¼ **pt**/3 cups asparagus liquor for simmering	
25 g/**1 oz** butter	
juice of 1 lemon	
a few drops of Worcestershire sauce	
1 onion, studded with cloves	
salt and freshly ground black pepper	
1 dish Cocktail Sauce (p10)	
1 dish Lemon Sauce (p17)	
1 dish Herb Cream (p13)	
1 dish melted butter	
1 dish chopped herbs	

1 Cut the meats into thin slices or cubes.
2 Cut the asparagus into bite-sized pieces.
3 Bring the wine and asparagus liquor to the boil in the fondue pot.
4 Add the butter, lemon juice, Worcester sauce and onion and simmer for 5 to 8 minutes. Season.
5 Arrange the meat, asparagus and side dishes on serving plates and serve with the stock.

Photograph (right)

Wine Fondue

Serves 4
Preparation time: 45 mins
1050 kcal/4410 kJ

150 g/*5 oz* veal fillet

150 g/*5 oz* turkey breast

150 g/*5 oz* goose breast

150 g/*5 oz* venison fillet

4 carrots, sliced

200 g/*7 oz* broccoli florets

500 ml/*18 fl oz/2¹/₄ cups* dry white wine

500 ml/*18 fl oz/2¹/₄ cups* meat stock for simmering

2 bay leaves

a few cloves

a few peppercorns

1 sprig of thyme

1 sprig of tarragon

salt and freshly ground black pepper

1 dish Lemon Sauce (p17)

1 dish Herb Cream (p13)

1 dish Cranberry Cream (p15)

1 dish chopped nuts

1 Cut the meat into thin strips or small cubes.
2 Blanch the vegetables in boiling salted water, then drain.
3 Pour the wine and stock into the fondue pot, add the spices and the herbs and simmer over a moderate heat for 5 to 8 minutes. Remove the sprigs of herbs and season to taste.
4 Arrange the meat, vegetables and side dishes on serving plates and serve with the stock.

Photograph (left)

Herb Fondue

Serves 4
Preparation time: 45 mins
760 kcal/3190 kJ

150 g/*5 oz* beef fillet

150 g/*5 oz* rabbit fillet

150 g/*5 oz* chicken breast fillet

150 g/*5 oz* cauliflower florets

150 g/*5 oz* broccoli florets

150 g/*5 oz* asparagus, cut into short lengths

750 ml/*1¹/₄ pt/3 cups* meat stock for simmering

250 ml/*8 fl oz/1 cup* dry white wine

2 onions, studded with cloves

1 sprig each of thyme, tarragon, basil, oregano

2 cloves garlic, chopped

1 dish Herb Cream (p13)

1 dish Dill Cream (p11)

1 dish Horseradish Sauce (p14)

1 dish Tzatziki (p17)

1 dish Egg Sauce (p11)

1 dish chopped herbs

1 Cut the meat into strips or cubes.
2 Quickly blanch the vegetables in boiling salted water, then drain.
3 Put the stock, wine, onion, herbs and garlic into the fondue pot and simmer over a moderate heat for 5 to 8 minutes. Remove the herbs.
4 Arrange the meat, vegetables and side dishes on serving plates and serve with the stock.

Photograph (right)

Paris Fondue

Serves 4
Preparation time: 55 mins
2540 kcal/10670 kJ

150 g/*5 oz* beef fillet
150 g/*5 oz* venison fillet
150 g/*5 oz* lamb fillet
100 g/*4 oz* broccoli florets
100 g/*4 oz* carrots
100 g/*4 oz* asparagus tips
100 g/*4 oz* spring onions
8-12 stuffed vine leaves
250 ml/*8 fl oz*/1 cup sparkling wine
500 ml/*18 fl oz*/2¹/₄ cups meat stock for simmering
150 ml/*¹/₄ pt*/²/₃ cup cream
2 sprigs of tarragon
a pinch of saffron strands
salt and freshly ground black pepper
1 dish Pineapple Foam (p10)
1 dish Fine Herb Sauce (p14)
1 dish Brandied Cranberries (p17)
1 dish Cocktail Sauce (p10)
1 dish Egg Sauce (p11)
1 dish Pepper Sauce (p14)

1 Dice the meat and blanch the vegetables.
2 Put the wine into the fondue pot. Add the stock, cream, herbs and saffron. Bring to the boil and simmer for 5 minutes. Remove the herb sprigs and season to taste.
3 Arrange the dishes on plates and serve with the stock.

Photograph opposite (top)

Forester's Fondue

Serves 4
Preparation time: 55 mins
2930 kcal/12395 kJ

150 g/*5 oz* venison fillet
300 g/*10 oz* pork fillet
150 g/*5 oz* gammon
150 g/*5 oz* mushrooms, diced
1 bunch of spring onions, cut into pieces
1 glass dry red wine
500 ml/*18 fl oz*/2¹/₄ cups meat stock for simmering
150 ml/*¹/₄ pt*/²/₃ cup whipping cream
30 ml/*2 tbsp* cranberry jelly
1 sprig of marjoram
1 sprig of thyme
15 ml/*1 tbsp* grated blue vein cheese
salt and freshly ground black pepper
1 dish Brandied Cranberries (p17)
1 dish Fine Herb Sauce (p14)
1 dish Bacon Sauce (p16)
1 dish chopped onions

1 Cube the meat.
2 Put the wine, stock, cream, cranberry jelly, herbs and blue cheese into the fondue pot, bring to the boil, stirring, and leave to stand for 5 minutes. Remove the herbs and season to taste with salt and pepper.
3 Arrange the meats, vegetables and side dishes on serving plates and serve with the stock.

Photograph opposite (bottom left)

Tomato Fondue

Serves 4
Preparation time: 50 mins
1850 kcal/7770 kJ

150 g/*5 oz* pork fillet
150 g/*5 oz* rump steak
150 g/*5 oz* turkey breast
4 frankfurters
1 white radish, diced
1 red pepper, diced
8-12 cherry tomatoes
300 ml/*¹/₂ pint* mixed vegetable juice (like V8)
1 glass red wine
600 ml/*1 pint*/2¹/₂ cups meat stock for simmering
2 cloves garlic
5 ml/*1 tsp* salt
1 sprig of thyme
1 sprig of marjoram
salt and freshly ground black pepper
1 dish Lemon Sauce (p17)
1 dish Horseradish Sauce (p14)
1 dish Remoulade Sauce (p15)
1 dish chopped nuts

1 Cut the meat and sausages into pieces and prepare the vegetables.
2 Bring the juice, wine and stock to the boil in the fondue pot. Add the garlic, salt and herbs and simmer for 8 minutes. Remove the herb sprigs and season to taste.
3 Arrange the meat, vegetables and side dishes on serving plates and serve with the stock.

Photograph opposite (bottom right)

Piquant Fondue

Serves 4
Preparation time: 50 mins
2040 kcal/8570 kJ

200 g/7 oz beef fillet

200 g/7 oz pheasant breast fillet

200 g/7 oz uncooked gammon

100 g/4 oz broccoli florets

100 g/4 oz asparagus, cut into pieces

100 g/4 oz mangetout

8-10 cherry tomatoes

25 g/1 oz/2 tbsp butter

1 clove garlic, chopped

1 onion, chopped

1 large tin chopped tomatoes

250 ml/8 fl oz/1 cup meat stock for simmering

1 sprig of oregano

1 sprig of basil

30 ml/2 tbsp grated Parmesan cheese

5 ml/1 tsp grated lemon rind

salt and freshly ground black pepper

1 dish Horseradish Sauce (p14)

1 dish Roquefort Sauce (p15)

1 dish Cocktail Sauce (p10)

1 dish Chive Sauce (p16)

1 Cut the meat, pheasant and gammon into thin slices or cubes.
2 Blanch the vegetables quickly in boiling salted water, then drain well. Wash and dry the tomatoes.
3 Heat the butter in the fondue pot, add the garlic and onion and fry lightly until pale gold. Add the tomatoes, stock and herbs and simmer over a moderate heat for 5 to 8 minutes. Remove the herbs.
4 Stir in the Parmesan cheese and lemon peel and season to taste with salt and pepper.
5 Arrange the meats, vegetables, tomatoes and side dishes on serving plates and serve with the stock.

Photograph opposite (top)

Cheese-Cream Fondue

Serves 4
Preparation time: 45 mins
2030 kcal/8525 kJ

150 g/5 oz chicken breast, boned

150 g/5 oz pork fillet

150 g/5 oz veal fillet

150 g/5 oz calves' liver

100 g/4 oz broccoli florets

100 g/4 oz cauliflower florets

100 g/4 oz celery sticks cut into pieces

8-12 cherry tomatoes

1 glass dry white wine

750 ml/1¼ pt/3 cups chicken stock for simmering

150 ml/¼ pt/⅔ cup whipping cream

30 ml/2 tbsp grated Parmesan cheese

1 sprig of oregano

1 sprig of basil

salt and freshly ground black pepper

1 dish Lemon Sauce (p17)

1 dish Pepper Sauce (p14)

1 dish Curry Sauce (p10)

1 Cut the chicken, pork, veal and liver into strips.
2 Blanch the vegetables and wash the tomatoes.
3 Pour the wine, stock and cream into the fondue pot and bring to the boil.
4 Fold in the Parmesan cheese and herbs and leave to stand for 5 minutes. Remove the herbs and season to taste with salt and pepper.
5 Arrange the meat, vegetables, tomatoes and side dishes on serving plates and serve with the stock.

Photograph opposite (bottom)

German Offal Fondue

Serves 4
Preparation time: 50 mins
1840 kcal/7730 kJ

150 g/5 oz veal kidney
150 g/5 oz pork liver
150 g/5 oz chicken liver
150 g/5 oz veal sweetbreads, blanched
225g/8 oz mushrooms
juice of 1 lemon
1 bunch of spring onions, cut into pieces
200 g/7 oz small carrots, blanched
300 ml/¹/₂ pt/1¹/₄ cups meat stock for simmering
150 ml/¹/₄ pt/²/₃ cup whipping cream
1 glass dry white wine
1 sprig of thyme
1 sprig of tarragon
1 dish Chive Sauce (p16)
1 dish Cocktail Sauce (p10)
1 dish Remoulade Sauce (p15)

1 Cut the prepared offal into cubes.
2 Sprinkle the mushrooms with lemon juice and prepare the vegetables.
3 Pour the stock into the fondue pot with the cream, wine and herbs. Bring to the boil and simmer over a moderate heat for 5 minutes. Remove the herbs.
4 Arrange the meat, vegetables and side dishes on serving plates and serve with the stock.

Photograph (left)

Garden Fondue

Serves 4
Preparation time: 50 mins
2040 kcal/8570 kJ

150 g/**5 oz** broccoli florets
150 g/**5 oz** cauliflower florets
4 carrots, sliced
1 stick celery, diced
4 small onions, diced
450 g/**1 lb** beef fillet
1 glass dry white wine
500 ml/**18 fl oz**/2$^1/_4$ cups vegetable stock for simmering
1 sprig of oregano
1 sprig of basil
150 ml/$^1/_4$ **pt**/$^2/_3$ cup cream
15 ml/**1 tbsp** cornflour
a few drops of lemon juice
salt and freshly ground black pepper
1 dish Fine Herb Sauce (p14)
1 dish Lemon Sauce (p17)
1 dish Horseradish Sauce (p14)

1 Blanch the vegetables in boiling salted water, then drain well. Cut the beef into strips.
2 Pour the wine and stock into the fondue pot. Add the herbs, bring to the boil and simmer for 5 to 8 minutes, then remove herbs.
3 Mix together the cream and cornflour, add to the stock and boil gently until thickened. Add the lemon juice and season to taste.
4 Arrange the vegetables, meat and side dishes on serving plates and serve with the stock.

Photograph (right)

Witches' Fondue

Serves 4
Preparation time: 50 mins
1390 kcal/5840 kJ

---

150 g/5 oz beef fillet

150 g/5 oz veal fillet

150 g/5 oz pork fillet

150 g/5 oz lobster tails

juice of 1 lemon

*a few drops of
Worcestershire sauce*

a few drops of brandy

*400 g/14 oz vegetables
(celery, carrots, leek), diced*

1 glass dry white wine

*750 ml/1¼ pt/3 cups meat
stock for simmering*

60 ml/4 tbsp medium sherry

*1 onion, studded with
cloves*

1 sprig of dill

1 sprig of tarragon

1 dish Dill Cream (p11)

1 dish Mustard Sauce (p16)

1 dish Caviar Sauce (p12)

*1 dish Remoulade Sauce
(p15)*

1 dish mixed pickles

1 Cut the meat into cubes. Sprinkle the lobster tails with lemon juice, Worcestershire sauce and brandy.
2 Blanch the vegetables in boiling salted water.
3 Pour the wine, stock and sherry into the fondue pot. Add the studded onion and the herbs then bring to the boil and leave to stand for 5 minutes. Remove the herbs.
4 Arrange the meat, lobster tails, vegetables and side dishes on serving plates and serve with the stock.

Gourmet Tip
To make a good stock essential for a successful fondue, boil up 450 g/1 lb diced beef shin in 2 l/3½ pt/8½ cups water. Add herbs (parsley, coriander and celery leaves), a few beef bones, 3 onions, 4 carrots, 2 cloves, 6 juniper berries, 2 bay leaves and 5 ml/1 tsp peppercorns. Skim while boiling. reduce the heat, add 30 ml/2 tbsp salt to taste and simmer, covered, for 2 hours. Strain before use.

Surf and Turf Speciality Fondue

Serves 4
Preparation time: 55 mins
1310 kcal/5500 kJ

150 g/**5 oz** beef fillet

150 g/**5 oz** pork fillet

150 g/**5 oz** veal kidneys

150 g/**5 oz** sole or halibut fillet

juice of 1 lemon

a few drops of Worcestershire sauce

4 carrots, sliced

1 stick celery, diced

1 small leek, sliced

2 onions, diced

1 glass dry white wine

120 ml/**4 fl oz**/¹/₂ cup fruit vinegar

750 ml/1¹/₄ **pt**/3 cups meat stock for simmering

1 onion, studded with cloves

1 sprig of thyme

1 sprig of chervil

salt and freshly ground black pepper

1 dish Dill Cream (p11)

1 dish Horseradish Sauce (p14)

1 dish Curry Sauce (p10)

1 dish Mustard Sauce (p16)

1 dish Pepper Sauce (p14)

1 Cut the beef, pork, kidneys and fish into cubes. Sprinkle the fish with lemon juice and Worcestershire sauce.
2 Blanch the carrots, celery and leek in boiling salted water then drain well.
3 Put the wine, the fruit vinegar, stock, studded onion and herbs into the fondue pot and simmer over a moderate heat for 5 to 8 minutes. Remove the sprigs of herbs and season to taste with salt and pepper.
4 Arrange the meat, fish, vegetables and side dishes on serving plates and serve with the stock.

Photograph opposite (top)

Starter Fondue

Serves 4
Preparation time: 40 mins
2470 kcal/11215 kJ

100 g/**4 oz** beef fillet

100 g/**4 oz** uncooked gammon

100 g/**4 oz** monkfish

2 smoked trout fillets

1 glass Champagne or sparkling wine

250 ml/**8 fl oz**/1 cup meat stock for simmering

150 ml/¹/₄ **pt**/²/₃ cup whipping cream

15 ml/**1 tbsp** grated Parmesan cheese

1 sprig of tarragon

1 sprig of chervil

a pinch of sugar

a pinch of nutmeg

salt and freshly ground black pepper

1 dish Caviar Sauce (p12)

1 dish Cocktail Sauce (p10)

1 dish Herb Cream (p13)

1 Cut the beef, gammon and fish into thin strips or cubes.
2 Put the Champagne or sparkling wine into the fondue pot with the stock, cream, Parmesan cheese, herbs and sugar. Bring to the boil and leave to stand for 5 minutes. Remove the herbs and season with nutmeg and salt and pepper.
3 Arrange the meats, fish and side dishes on serving plates and serve with the stock.

Photograph opposite (bottom)

Unusual Fondue Dishes

Fondues are cooked all over the world and there are many delicious dishes with an international flavour which you can savour.

Indonesian Kebab Fondue, page 56

Indonesian Kebab Fondue

Serves 4
Preparation time: 55 mins
plus marinating
1560 kcal/6550 kJ

---

200 g/*7 oz* pork fillet

---

200 g/*7 oz* chicken breast fillet

---

200 g/*7 oz* duck breast fillet

8-12 lobster tails

---

1 small pineapple, peeled and cubed

---

1 banana, cubed

---

1 Spanish onion, cubed

---

a few drops of lemon juice

---

2 courgettes, sliced

---

200 g/*7 oz* mushrooms

---

250 ml/*8 fl oz*/1 cup dry sherry

---

120 ml/*4 fl oz*/*1/2* cup olive oil

---

120 ml/*4 fl oz*/*1/2* cup fruit vinegar

---

2 cloves garlic, chopped

---

5 ml/*1 tsp* paprika

---

10 ml/*2 tsp* grated ginger root

---

1 dish Curry Sauce (p10)

---

1 dish Chive Sauce (p16)

---

1 dish chopped peanuts

---

1 dish soy sauce

---

oil or vegetable fat for frying

---

1 Cut the meats into cubes and shell the lobster tails.
2 Arrange the meat, lobster tails, fruit, onion, courgettes and mushrooms on small wooden skewers. Sprinkle with lemon juice.

3 Mix together the sherry, olive oil, fruit vinegar, garlic, paprika and ginger. Pour over the Kebabs, cover and leave to marinate for at least 1 hour in the refrigerator, turning occasionally.
4 Arrange the kebabs and side dishes on serving plates. Heat the oil, pour it into the fondue pot, and serve.

Photograph page 54

Gourmet Tip
A speciality of Indonesian cuisine is peanut sauce. It is served with many dishes and also features in our Indonesian kebabs as a piquant addition. To make peanut sauce, purée about 225 g/8 oz/1 cup of salted peanuts, 5 ml/*1/2* tsp cayenne pepper and 250 ml/8 fl oz/1 cup of meat or chicken stock. Bring the purée slowly to the boil and thicken with cornflour according to taste. The sauce can be refined a little with soy or oyster sauce, honey and tomato ketchup or simply with crème fraîche. Serve the sauce warm or cold.

Fondue for Connoisseurs

Serves 4
Preparation time: 35 mins
2640 kcal/11090 kJ

8-12 slices fillet of hare

8-12 lamb chops

---

250 ml/8 fl oz/1 cup olive oil

---

salt and freshly ground black pepper

---

30 ml/2 tbsp honey

---

15 ml/1 tbsp wine vinegar

---

1 clove garlic, crushed

---

grated rind of 1/2 lemon

---

5 ml/1 tsp ground peppercorns

---

5 ml/1 tsp crushed juniper berries

---

5 ml/1 tsp chopped marjoram

---

5 ml/1 tsp chopped thyme

---

1 dish Fine Herb Sauce (p14)

---

1 dish Brandied Cranberries (p17)

---

1 dish Cocktail Sauce (p10)

---

oil or vegetable fat for frying

---

1 Cut the meat into cubes and place in a bowl.
2 Mix together the oil, salt and pepper, honey, wine vinegar, garlic, lemon rind, peppercorns, juniper berries and herbs, to make a marinade.
3 Pour over the meat, cover and leave in the refrigerator for 6 to 8 hours, turning occasionally.
4 Arrange the meat and side dishes on serving plates. Heat the oil, pour it into the fondue pot, and serve.

Photograph opposite

Baked Fondue Speciality

Serves 4
Preparation time: 35 mins
2870 kcal/12050 kJ

100 g/4 oz broccoli florets
100 g/4 oz cauliflower florets
100 g/4 oz Brussels sprouts
100 g/4 oz carrots, diced
200 g/7 oz pork fillet
200 g/7 oz beef fillet
200 g/7 oz lamb fillet
2 cloves garlic, crushed
5 ml/1 tsp salt
250 ml/8 fl oz/1 cup olive oil
1 onion, grated
10 ml/2 tsp green peppercorns
10 ml/2 tsp herbs de Provence
250 g/9 oz plain flour
250 ml/8 fl oz/1 cup milk
2 eggs separated
grated rind of ¹/₂ lemon
a pinch of salt
1 dish Cocktail Sauce (p10)
1 dish Egg Sauce (p11)
1 dish Herb Cream (p13)
1 dish Pepper Sauce (p14)
oil or vegetable fat for frying

1 Blanch the vegetables in boiling salted water for 6 to 8 minutes. Drain.
2 Cut the meat into cubes and place in a bowl.
3 Mix together the garlic, salt, olive oil, onion, peppercorns and herbs to make a marinade.
4 Pour the marinade over the meats and mix thoroughly. Leave in the refrigerator for at least 3 to 4 hours, turning occasionally.
5 Sieve the flour into a bowl. Beat in the milk, egg yolks, lemon rind and salt. Continue beating until completely smooth.
6 Whisk the egg whites until stiff and fold into the batter.
7 Arrange the batter and side dishes on serving plates. Heat the oil, pour it into the fondue pot, and serve.
8 To eat, spear vegetables or meat on the fondue forks, immerse in the batter and then hold in the hot fat until cooked to taste.

Chinese Fondue

Serves 4
Preparation time: 35 mins
880 kcal/3695 kJ

---

100 g/*4 oz* beef fillet

100 g/*4 oz* veal fillet

100 g/*4 oz* duck breast fillet

100 g/*4 oz* veal liver

100 g/*4 oz* veal kidney

100 g/*4 oz* mushrooms sliced

100 g/*4 oz* carrots, cut into strips

100 g/*4 oz* broccoli florets, blanched

100 g/*4 oz* swede, cut into strips

100 g/*4 oz* bean sprouts

1 litre/1³/4 **pts**/4¹/4 cups chicken stock for simmering

1 clove garlic, chopped

10 ml/**2 tsp** grated ginger root

120 ml/**4 fl oz**/¹/₂ cup fruit vinegar

120 ml/**4 fl oz**/¹/₂ cup soy sauce

20 ml/**4 tsp** honey

1 dish Crab Cream (p13)

1 dish Tangy Honey and Tomato Sauce (p12)

1 dish Chinese Garlic Sauce (p13)

---

1 Cut the meat, liver and kidneys into slices or strips.
2 Arrange them decoratively in serving dishes with the vegetables and bean sprouts.
3 Pour the stock into the fondue pot. Add the garlic, ginger, fruit vinegar, soy sauce and honey and simmer on a moderate heat for 5 to 8 minutes.
4 Arrange the serving dishes of meat and vegetables and the side dishes and serve with the stock.
5 Place the food in frying baskets to cook in the stock.

Gourmet Tip
For authenticity, provide the diners with chopsticks and Chinese-style crockery to complete the atmosphere. These and the frying baskets can be obtained from cookshops or Chinese supermarkets.

Hong Kong Meat Fondue

Serves 4
Preparation time: 35 mins
1850 kcal/7770 kJ

300 g/11 *oz* pork fillet
300 g/11 *oz* pigs' liver
1 red pepper, diced
1 green pepper, diced
1 bunch of spring onions, cut into pieces
100 g/4 *oz* swede, diced
100 g/4 *oz* lychees
100 g/4 *oz* pineapple, cubed
100 g/4 *oz* mangos, cubed
500 ml/18 fl oz/2¹/₂ cups meat stock for simmering
120 ml/4 fl oz/¹/₂ cup soy sauce
250 ml/8 fl oz/1 cup rice wine
15 ml/1 *tbsp* tomato purée
15 ml/1 *tbsp* honey
60 ml/4 *tbsp* oyster sauce
a pinch of saffron strands
salt and freshly ground black pepper
1 dish soy sauce
1 dish chopped nuts

1 Cut the meat and liver into cubes and arrange decoratively on small dishes with the vegetables and fruit.
2 Mix the stock with the soy sauce, rice wine, tomato purée, honey, oyster sauce and saffron and simmer over a moderate heat in the fondue pot for 5 to 8 minutes. Season to taste, with salt and pepper.

3 Arrange the dishes of meat and vegetables and the side dishes and serve with the stock.
4 Place the food in frying baskets to cook in the stock.

Photograph opposite (top)

Mongolian Mix

Serves 4
Preparation time: 25 mins
2170 kcal/9115 kJ

150 g/5 *oz* goose breast fillet
150 g/5 *oz* duck breast fillet
150 g/5 *oz* pork fillet
100 g/4 *oz* bamboo shoots
100 g/4 *oz* broccoli florets
200 g/7 *oz* transparent noodles, pre-cooked
750 ml/1¹/₄ *pts*/3 cups chicken stock for simmering
120 ml/4 fl oz/¹/₂ cup hoisin sauce
2 cloves garlic, chopped
250 ml/8 fl oz/1 cup medium sherry
120 ml/4 fl oz/¹/₂ cup fruit vinegar
small red pepper pod, seeds removed and chopped
salt and freshly ground black pepper
1 dish Pineapple Foam (p10)
1 dish Curry Sauce (p10)

1 Cut the fillets into thin slices.
2 Wash the shoots and the vegetables, drain well and arrange decoratively with the meat and noodles in small dishes.
3 Put the stock, hoisin sauce, garlic, sherry, fruit vinegar and pepper pod into a fondue pot and simmer over a moderate heat for 5 to 8 minutes. Season to taste with salt and pepper.
4 Arrange the serving dishes of meat and vegetable with the side dishes and serve with the stock.
5 Cook the food in frying baskets.

Photograph opposite (bottom)

Gourmet Tip
As in the case of all Asian dishes, the ingredients are cut into either strips, diamond-shaped pieces, squares or slices. Depending on the kind of ingredients, the produce should be cut into a size that will ensure an identical cooking time for all. If this is not possible, some ingredients should be pre-cooked in oil.

Index of Recipes

Foulsham
Yeovil Road, Slough, Berkshire, SL1 4JH
ISBN 0-572-01723-5
This English language edition copyright
© 1992 W. Foulsham & Co. Ltd.
Originally published by Falken-Verlag,
GmbH, Niedernhausen TS, West
Germany.
Photographs copyright © Falken-Verlag.

All rights reserved.
The Copyright Act (1956) prohibits
(subject to certain very limited
exceptions) the making of copies of any
copyright work or of a substantial part of
such a work, including the making of
copies by photocopying or similar
process. Written permission to make a
copy or copies must therefore normally
be obtained from the publisher in
advance. It is advisable also to consult
the publisher if in any doubt as to the
legality of any copying which is to be
undertaken.

Printed in Portugal